Being a Knight
for
King Jesus

A study of Ephesians 6
for children ages 8-12

Shawn Lamb

Illustrations by Robert and Briana Lamb

Being a Knight for King Jesus
A Study of Ephesians 6 for Children Ages 8-12

by Shawn Lamb

Published by Allon Books
209 Hickory Way Court
Antioch, Tennessee 37013
www.allonbooks.com

Character illustrations by Briana Lamb

Armor illustrations and cover design by Robert Lamb

International Standard Book Number: 979-0-9891029-7-1

Preface

Kids ages 8-12 will enjoy this short study of Ephesians 6. Prince Nigel and his wife, Princess Mirit, from the biblical allegorical series Allon, talk about the armor of God.

As The King's Champion, Nigel tells the proper use of the individual pieces of armor. He shares his knowledge on the importance of spiritual life to a knight.

Mirit shares her husband duties much like Priscilla helped Aquila in supporting Paul in Acts 18. She provides her insights from past experience.

Together, they challenge kids to become a Knight of The King.

Prince Nigel
The King's Champion

To Be a Knight of the King

Training to be a knight is very hard work. It takes patience, diligence and commitment to learn what is required. Most of all, it takes faith and trust; Faith in God's calling, and trust that He will enable you to fulfill that calling. Only then can each piece of the armor be properly used.

It took years before I earned my right to be called The King's Champion. With the right training, you too can become a champion knight of King Jesus.

The Bible says,

Be diligent to present yourself approved to God as a workman who does not need to be ashamed, rightly handling the word of truth.

2 Timothy 2:15
NKJV

Being diligent means to be constantly practicing to be good at something. Whenever I present myself to the King, I make certain everything on my uniform is in good order. I have all my weapons in readiness for whatever the King commands. More than that, I also come with a willingness of mind and spirit to obey.

My armor can only protect me so much, if my mind and spirit aren't willing to do what the King wants. So as we look at the different pieces of a knight's armor, I'll remind you about your attitude and heart. No one can engage in battle without being sure in mind.

Nigel's right. Since a child, I learned how to fight with a sword. However, it wasn't until I married Nigel that I understood what it meant to use my sword properly.

A sword isn't just for fighting. A sword must be used with knowledge and precision in order to be effective. Once I learned how to use my sword in the right way, I became a more complete warrior.

The greatest lesson I learned is patience. I had to stop being eager to engage anyone and everyone, or do what I wanted.

Princess Mirit
The Queen's Champion

Let patience have perfect work, that you may be perfect and entire, lacking nothing.

James 1:4
KJV

Sounds hard to be perfect right?

The Bible doesn't mean doing everything right. It means to improve in moral character—be a better person, a better knight. This means I only use my sword when necessary, in defense of the King and not for myself. Learning these lessons helped me become a happier and more content person.

The Armor of God

The best passage in the Bible for describing armor is Ephesians 6. Let's look at verses 10 and 11 to understand why you must have your armor on and in good working order.

... be strong in the Lord and in the strength of his might. Put on the whole armor of God, that you may be able to stand against the schemes of the devil.

Ephesians 6:10-11
ESV

When studying to become a knight, I spent many hours learning to nurture my spiritual mind and heart. It became important for me never to do anything without prayer, because the devil is a powerful enemy.

As Ephesians 6:10 says, it is the strength of King Jesus, which helps to keep your armor ready.

Another verse in the Bible also states the importance of staying strong with King Jesus.

> *Be sober-minded; be watchful. Your adversary the devil prowls around like a roaring lion seeking someone to devour.*
>
> **1 Peter 5:8**
> **ESV**

If I'm not prepared in my mind and spirit, I can easily be tricked or distracted. When that happens, I can fail my king by not doing what I should.

Putting on the armor and being ready to serve King Jesus needs a clear (sober) mind and true heart.

Can you think of ways the devil tricks you? Do you know how to deal with failure when it happens?

It's easy to feel bad after doing something wrong. But you don't need to hold onto sorrow and regret. King Jesus is ready and willing to forgive, if you ask him.

If we confess our sins, he is faithful and just to forgive us our sins and to cleanse us from all unrighteousness.

1 John 1:9
ESV

The virtue of a knight is the greatest weapon. When one asks King Jesus for a clean heart and pure mind, the Bible says the knight can resist the enemy and he will flee.

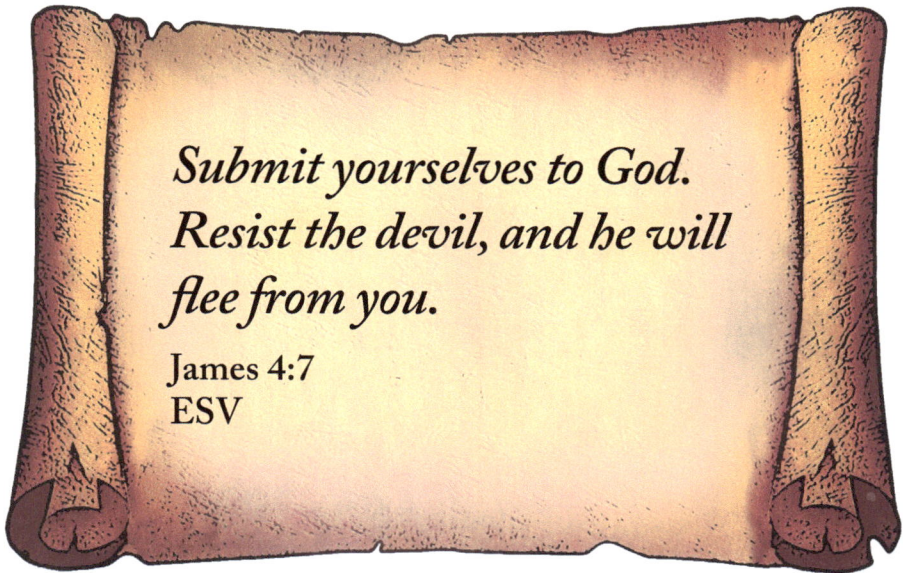

Submit yourselves to God. Resist the devil, and he will flee from you.

James 4:7
ESV

To submit means to obey. A knight is quick to follow orders.

TRUTH

Stand, having fastened on the belt of truth, and having put on the breastplate of righteousness.

**Ephesians 6:14
ESV**

The Belt of Truth

Knights can't fight very well sitting down. The first thing I learned was how to stand properly so I could keep my balance. The word *stand* or *standfast* is found almost 300 times in the Bible. It is very important to know how to stay on your feet. If you stand in the strength of King Jesus, the devil can't easily knock you down.

Very often the belt is neglected, because many think of it as a small piece that is not essential to the sword. But it is! Truth is what makes the belt very important to the sword.

Pontius Pilate asked Jesus what is truth? We know the answer to that question. King Jesus said it best:

I am the way, the truth and the life.

John 14:6
NKJV

> *Sanctify them in truth; your word is truth.*
>
> **John 17:17**
> **NKJV**

God's word is truth, and King Jesus is the expression of that truth. The belt goes around the waist to hold The Truth and sword together.

I don't have to go looking for my sword when danger happens. All I do is reach to my side and draw my sword, while the Truth wraps around me to give me the strength to stand.

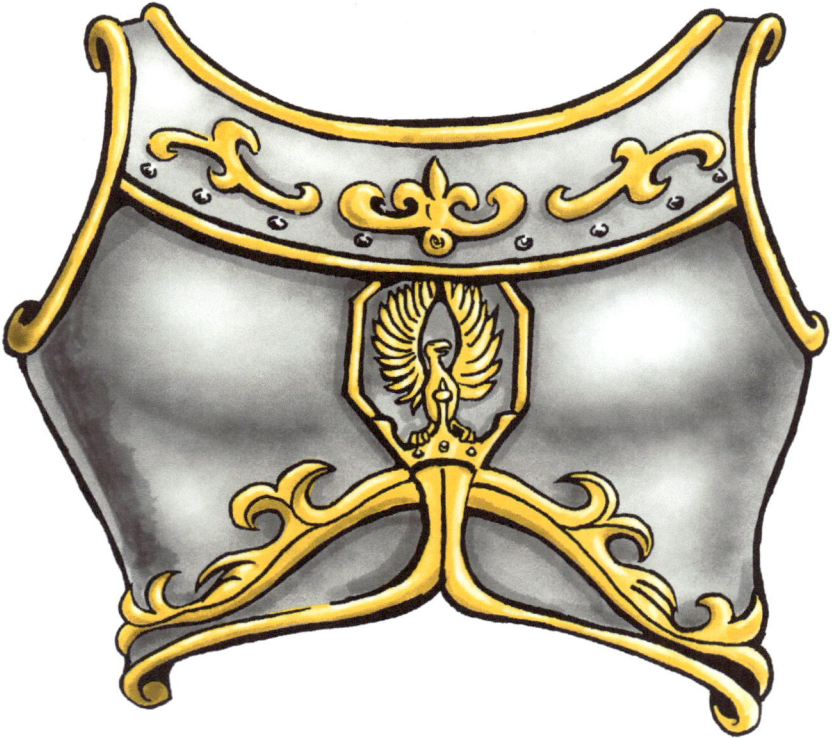

... having put on the breastplate of righteousness.

Ephesians 6:14
NKJV

The Breastplate of Righteousness

For a knight, the breastplate covers the heart. The heart is what keeps everyone alive! It needs strong protection.

The breastplate of a knight must be kept in good working order. Never allow it to get rusty or broken. This makes the breastplate weak and unable to withstand any attack. Dings in armor are signs of a well-fought battle, but need to be repaired and kept strong for the next skirmish.

The same can be said for the spiritual heart of a knight. As a Christian, King Jesus gave you a new spiritual heart and warns you to protect it.

Above all else, guard your heart, for everything you do flows from it.

Proverbs 4:23
NIV

Everything you do in life comes from the heart. What you say and how you treat others begins in the heart. Knowing the words of God and King Jesus is the best way to keep the righteous breastplate clean and in place.

> *Your word have I hidden in my heart that I might not sin against you.*
>
> **Psalms 119:11**
> **NKJV**

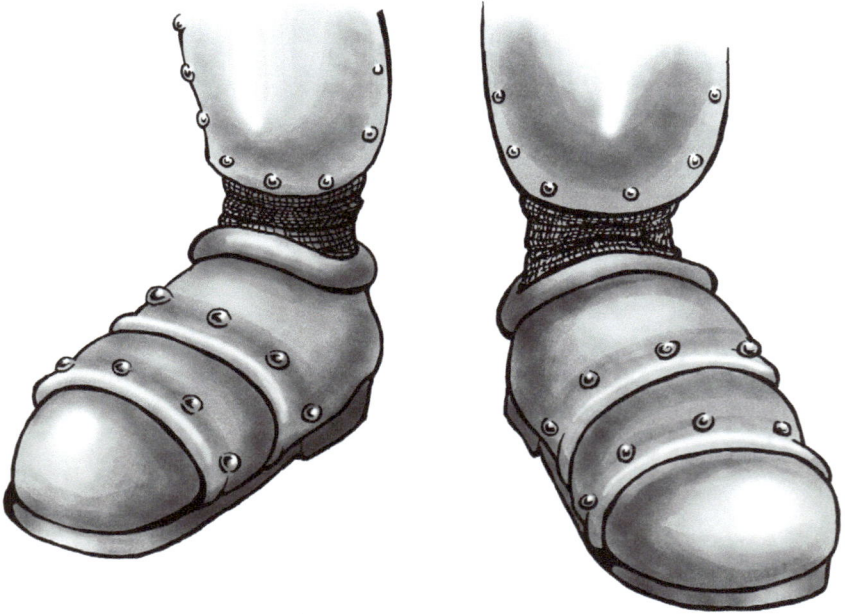

... and as shoes for your feet...

Ephesians 6:15
NKJV

The Shoes

Learning to keep my balance was helped
by having a good pair of shoes.

Fighting when barefoot hurts! One can step on rocks or slip in the mud, and this causes a distraction from battle. All my focus needs to be on the enemy and not when I step with bare feet.

The shoes of a knight were made of metal plates or thick leather boots. These protected the feet from being a target of the enemy. Shoes also helped the knight to move easily over rocky ground.

Has someone ever stepped on your bare foot? Yes, it can also hurt with a shoe on, but the harder the shoe, the less pain.

Just like the rest of the armor, the shoes need to be ready to either stand firm in place or move when King Jesus commands.

... having put on the readiness of the gospel of peace.

Ephesians 6:15
NKJV

The most important function of a knight is to defend. A knight doesn't go around looking for a fight. The strength of a knight is the ability to bring and keep *peace*.

Wherever I go in my travels, I represent my king. I bring my king's word to declare his will to the people. King Jesus asks you to do the same so that people can have *peace* with God.

> *That which we have seen and heard we proclaim also to you.*
>
> 1 John 1:3a
> NKJV

> *Go, therefore, and make disciples of all nations ...*
>
> Matthew 28:19
> NKJV

You shall be my witnesses in Jerusalem, Judea, Samaria, and to the ends of the earth.

Acts 1:8
NKJV

It is a knight's readiness to obey that makes him or her useful to the king.

The Shield of Faith

In all circumstances, take up the shield of faith, with which you can extinguish all the flaming darts of the evil one.

Ephesians 6:16
NKJV

A knight must be ready at all times to respond to danger and the king. One of the best tools for defense is a shield. These can come in many sizes, but the most effective one is large and can protect most of the body.

During times of war, I have faced flaming arrows (darts) and other projectiles. The shield serves as my first line of defense. When held strong, darts bounce off the shield, causing no damage.

Large shields can be heavy, but remember this is the first element to help you fight against the enemy:

Be strong in the Lord and in the strength of his might.

Ephesians 6:10
NKJV

With the strength of King Jesus you can hold the shield to protect yourself from *flaming darts of the evil one*.

The key to using the shield properly is *faith*. Nothing protects a spiritual knight as well as faith. It keeps the knight in place and ready to face any danger or respond to the king's command without question.

Remember the devil as a roaring lion mentioned in 1 Peter 5:8? Now read the next verse.

Resist him, firm in your faith.

1 Peter 5:9
NKJV

What will that *faithful resistance* of the enemy lead to? John tells us in his letter.

> *For everyone who has been born of God overcomes the world. And this is the victory that has overcome the world—your faith!*
>
> 1 John 5:4
> ESV

That's right! *Faith* can give you victory!

Take the helmet of salvation, and the sword of the spirit, which is the Word of God.

Ephesians 6:17
NKJV

The Helmet of Salvation

Next to the heart, the head is the most important part of the body that needs protection. It is where we think and where we place Scripture we memorize. It is also most vulnerable because of what we see and hear from the world around us.

I wouldn't go into battle without my helmet. I may be looking one way, when something comes from another direction aimed at my head.

How many times have you been doing something good and a bad thought comes to mind? You know it's a wrong thought, so what can you do?

There is a song we teach little children called "O, Be Careful Little Eyes." Perhaps you have heard of it. If not, it goes like this:

O be careful little eyes what you see.
O be careful little eyes what you see.
There's a Father up above
And He's looking down in love.
So, be careful little eyes what you see.

O be careful little ears what you hear.
O be careful little ears what you hear.
There's a Father up above
And He's looking down in love.
So, be careful little ears what you hear.

King Jesus knows what you see, hear and do. He's given you the *helmet of salvation* to protect your mind, get rid of the bad thoughts and keep them from causing trouble.

Take the helmet of salvation, and the sword of the spirit, which is the Word of God.

Ephesians 6:17
NKJV

The Sword of the Spirit

Earlier Nigel said that a knight does not go looking for a fight. The most important duty is to defend. This is what I needed to learn, that the sword is mostly a weapon of defense. However, when used properly, the spiritual sword is a powerful weapon.

> *For the word of God is living and active, sharper than any two-edged sword, piercing to the division of soul and spirit, joints and marrow, to discerning the thoughts and intents of the heart.*
>
> **Hebrews 4:12**
> **ESV**

If you look at the list of pieces for the armor, the sword is the only weapon. The rest are used to protect the knight. Take the example of King Jesus from the Gospel of Luke in chapter four. After Jesus was baptized he went into the wilderness where the enemy tempted him. At each temptation, King Jesus replied with Scripture and the devil left.

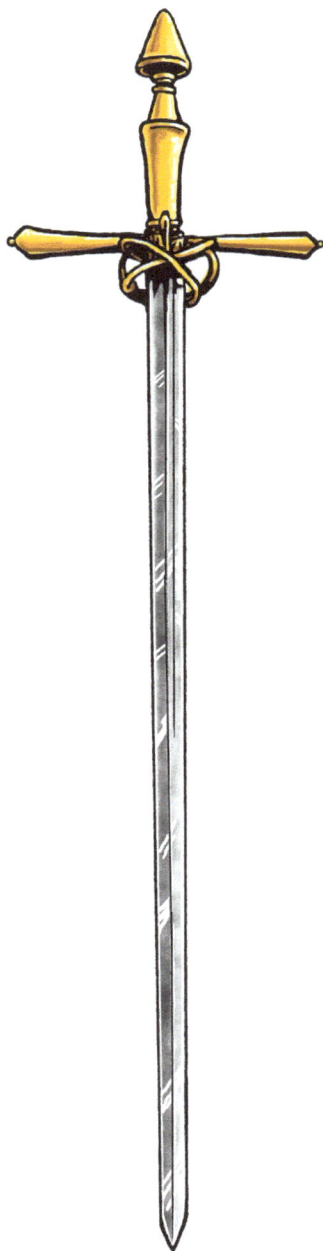

The Whole Armor of God

When the armor is assembled, and in perfect working order, the spiritual knight is able to face anything for King Jesus.

With faith in God, David faced Goliath and won! With that same faith, you can be victorious.

Remember, the enemy is relentless, so a knight must always be ready. Hiding God's word in your heart is the place to start. In fact, it is the Word of Truth that holds the armor together, and where the knight draws courage for the battle.

Have I not commanded you?
Be strong and courageous.
Do not be frightened, and
do not be dismayed, for the
LORD your God is with you
wherever you go.

Joshua 1:92
NKJV

Review Questions

1. Which piece of the armor protects the head?

2. The breastplate covers what part of the body?

3. Can you name a knight's weapon?

4. What part of the armor can stop flaming darts?

5. Name the smallest part of the armor, but is very important.

6. A knight wears these on the feet.

7. What does the whole armor help you do?

8. Who is the adversary?

9. Who does the knight obey?

Answers on page 53.

Finish the verse.

1. Take the_____of salvation and the
   _____which is the_____ of God.
   Ephesians 6:17

2. Be_____ in the Lord and in the
   _____ of his might.
   Ephesians 6:10

3. _____, having fastened on the
   _____ and having put on
   the _____ of _____
   Ephesians 6:14

4. And as _____ for your feet,
   having put on the readiness of the
   _____ of peace.
   Ephesians 6:15

5. Therefore take up the _____
   _____ of God, that you may be able
   to withstand in the _____ day,
   and having done all to _____
   Ephesians 6:13

6. Be sober-minded; be watchful. Your
   adversary the _____ prowls
   around like a _____
   seeking someone to devour.
   1 Peter 5:8

7. I am the way, the_____ and the life.
   John 14:6

8. Your _____ have I hidden in
   my _____ that I might not sin
   against you.
   Psalms 119:11

Answers to Review Questions

1. Which piece of the armor protects the head? **(helmet)**

2. The breastplate covers what part of the body? **(heart)**

3. Can you name a knight's weapon? **(sword)**

4. What part of the armor can stop flaming darts? **(shield)**

5. Name the smallest part of the armor, but is very important. **(belt)**

6. A knight wears these on the feet. **(shoes)**

7. What does the whole armor help you do? **(stand firm)**

8. Who is the adversary? **(the devil)**

9. Who does the knight obey? **(the King/King Jesus)**

Other Books by Shawn Lamb

Young Adult Fantasy Fiction
ALLON ~ BOOK 1
Published by Creation House, a division of Charisma Media

Published by Allon Books
ALLON ~ BOOK 2 ~ INSURRECTION
ALLON ~ BOOK 3 ~ HEIR APPARENT
ALLON ~ BOOK 4 ~ A QUESTION OF SOVEREIGNTY
ALLON ~ BOOK 5 ~ GAUNTLET
ALLON ~ BOOK 6 ~ DILEMMA
ALLON ~ BOOK 7 ~ DANGEROUS DECEPTION
ALLON ~ BOOK 8 ~ DIVIDED
ALLON ~ BOOK 9 ~ IN PLAIN SIGHT
PARENT STUDY GUIDE FOR ALLON ~ BOOKS 1-9
THE ACTIVITY BOOK OF ALLON

For Young Readers – ages 8–10
Allon ~ The King's Children series

NECIE AND THE APPLES
TRISTINE'S DORGIRITH ADVENTURE
NIGEL'S BROKEN PROMISE

Historical Fiction
GLENCOE
THE HUGUENOT SWORD

www.ingramcontent.com/pod-product-compliance
Lightning Source LLC
Chambersburg PA
CBHW041758040426
42447CB00001B/4